Save money and become a millionaire

Millionaire budget guidelines and investing for beginners to go from debt to very rich.

By

Marco Klee

"Formal education will make you a living; self-education will make you a fortune." --Jim Rohn

Content

Save money and become a millionaire 1

Learn from the people who became very rich by saving money 4

Why you should save 9

How to set a realistic savings target 11

How to lower your expenses 13

    Money sucking categories 14

    Savings Checklist 23

Saving in every life situation 24

Seductions that make saving more difficult 31

What you should do with the saved money 34

    Savings account 36

    Gold and Silver 37

    Real estate 38

    ETFs 40

    Shares of more well-known companies 42

    Lending loans 43

Final thoughts on investment 45

How to get more revenue in addition to investments 46

    Side job as an employee 47

    Secondary job as a self-employed person 47

Create a budget 48

    Monthly budget 49

Learn from the people who became very rich by saving money

Being rich, having a lot of money, and being financially free are very trendy topics on which there are countless books. Sure, everyone would like to know the secret with which you can become a millionaire as quick as possible and fulfill all your dreams. Such "tips" on fast wealth may work for the first few in a niche, but unfortunately everyone else usually loses money.

You may even have had a bad experience with false promises of quick money.

Saving is an area that most people would like to overlook. It sounds stingy and too strenuous. So why should you choose this book? Because that's what this is all about: getting rich by saving. There are several reasons why it was a good decision that you picked this book and not another one:

1. I live by this philosophy and it works

There are not only collected lists from the Internet in this book, but the savings tips are thoroughly tried and tested. The good thing is that the more the wealth grows, the faster it will become even bigger because you can safely invest some of the savings. At the age of 18, I had 30'000 Fr. in my account. Despite taking driver's ed, studying, and traveling in Australia and the Pacific Islands for 9 months, I had 100'000 Fr. on my savings account when I was 23. At 28, my fortune reached the 350'000 mark. So, I'm on the right track to half a million, and believe me, I'm enjoying my life to its fullest. This takes me to the next point.

2. You'll learn how to save without feeling that you've got to give up everything.

I was a bit of an extreme as a child what concerns money. I have no idea why I was so frugal as a kid because my family was typically middle class. Neither poor nor luxurious, but we had everything we needed and could afford regular holidays. So, there was no reason why I always put most of my pocket money in my piggy bank while my brother was buying sweets with his money. But somehow, I couldn't help it. I always felt that there were even better things to buy and that I wanted enough money to be able to afford them. From 15 to 24, this earned me the nickname bargain hunter, which was not necessarily positive in the eyes of others. When I was 25, I wanted to change something. It couldn't be that I had more money than all my friends, but (except extensive travel) I spent less money than them every month.

Maybe it is difficult for you to understand, but it was very hard for me to start spending more money. I had to force myself to treat myself to more Starbucks coffee or the more expensive pizza if I wanted to.

The great realization was that even though I felt like I had totally gone overboard this month, I was still saving more than I did the previous month. My saved (and invested) money had started to work for me. So, I told my conscience that I could afford more without being scared of going broke and people who newly met me would no longer call me a penny pincher.

I told you this little story of my life so that you understand that I really know how to save properly, but now I have learned that you don't have to give up everything to achieve your savings goals. A good middle way is realistic and will also bring you forward.

3. Saving money is the surest way toward owning a million

Did you know that most millionaires did not get rich through lucky investments, but through constant work and smart saving? The book "**The Millionaire Next Door**" by Dr. Thomas J. Stanley and Dr. William Danko states that the typical millionaire does not show how rich he/she is, because he/she chooses to live in a normal neighborhood and drive average cars. The people who are thought to be super-rich often live above their means and the wealth is short-lived.

This knowledge should now help a pleasant calmness to spread inside you. Because it means that your saved money will not put any pressure on you. You won't have to keep up with any expected standards. You can confidently enjoy your wealth by using it for things that are really important to you (traveling, dining in nice restaurants, or a sports car), but you don't have to prove how much money you have on all levels. While your environment is constantly worried about how they can get to the end of the next month and still afford their Zalando packages or technical innovations, you smile and look at your growing account balance.

4. Learn how to make the money work for you

Once you've saved your first ten thousand, you can make the money work for you and make even more profit. You don't have any pressure to make the quick buck and it would be a shame to lose a lot of money in the event of a malinvestment. That's why we're going to look at some investment opportunities that will grow your wealth in the long run.

Now you know, why reading this book will benefit you. So, if you're interested in becoming a millionaire, read on and dive into savings tips and the guaranteed growth of your wealth (in no time).

Why you should save

Before you decide to save, you need to set your reason why you save. The big goal may be to become a millionaire. It's a good goal because it will motivate you to save even more if you already have hundreds of thousands in your account. However, you should also have smaller goals so that you can see rapid progress and stay motivated.

Find your *WHYs*!

You may want to do further education which you have to pay for yourself, you might want to have a certain amount on your account before you start a family, you finally want to fly to Japan or South America, or you would like to buy a car or house. Whatever your small and intermediate goals are, write them down. Also, write down the number you want to see in your account when you want to fulfill the goals.

If you're at 0 at the moment and would like to receive a pay advance every month, it's not realistic that you will be at 200'000 in a year. But 20'000 to 40'000 are possible if you stick to the savings tips from this book.

Create a vision board

If you're a visual person, you can design a small vision board with your savings goals.
You cut out pictures of the desired items (e.g. car, pictures of beautiful beaches) or you draw something yourself and write down your desired fortune as a number. This way you can see your goal every day and you will be constantly guided by it.

Surely you have already thought about which savings goal you would like to achieve. Quickly look at the next chapter before you design your vision board to pick a realistic number. Of course, you may set your goal a bit higher, but the feeling of success will be much better if you set yourself a realistic goal and then see that your wealth is actually growing.

How to set a realistic savings target

If you're always at zero at the end of the month, you're obviously doing something wrong. No matter what life situation you are in, you should always be able to put at least **20 percent** of your salary aside. This is your goal if you are in debt at the moment or your account balance is less than 10'000. You're going to put 20 % of your income aside every month, no matter how much you earn. Now you can already calculate how much money this will bring you in 5 months. Even if it doesn't look like much, it's worth going through with it for the next two years. Because, as already mentioned, once you have a certain amount saved up, the money starts "having children".

If you're already good at saving, you can increase your savings rate by up to 50%. See what is possible for you. The more you save, the faster your wealth will grow.
If that's still too slow for you, you can make sure to create additional streams of income. We will also look at this topic in this book.

But back to your vision board. Design it and write down your fortune as a number that you want to reach on a certain date in the next two years. For example, 150'000 on July 31, 2022.

How to lower your expenses

The most important thing in order to get a better savings rate is to know what you're spending your money on in the first place. For this, I highly recommend using a budget app. I use **AndroMoney**. There, I can enter my income and expenses and nice charts show me what I spend my money on.

You just have to get used to entering each expense individually. Use categories such as snacks, dining out, groceries, rent, public transport, car, your hobbies, alcohol, travel, gifts, medical expenses, medicine, clothes, etc.

If you have an overview of your expenses, you can focus on the details you need to change to save money. As an advanced step, you can then create a budget plan that allows you to spend money in a relaxed way every month, and at the end of the month your calculations should work out.

Money sucking categories and how to minimize these expenses

Now let's take a look at some of these money-sucking categories and get tips on how to reduce spending in those categories. You probably can't focus on everything at the same time, otherwise, it's a little overwhelming. That's why you'll find a checklist of budget targets at the end of the chapter. Write a budget target per category for your monthly expenses and gradually focus on more categories. When you reach your budget goal, you can tick it off. You can also copy the list and hang it on your door or next to the Vision Board.

Alcohol and going out

If alcohol is a big cost for you, it would be beneficial to drastically reduce alcohol consumption. Above all: don't drink in bars or restaurants anymore. Drinks in bars and restaurants literally pull the money out of your pocket. Then, there is also a tip and perhaps you have to invite your friends from time to time. No! With good friends, you don't have to. Tell them about your savings goal and, if necessary, allow yourself a monthly budget that you can use for drinking outside of your apartment. Don't exceed that budget. Of course, it would be even better if you only enjoy drinks at home and buy alcohol in the cheapest shop you find. You can have friends over at home as well. Make sure that you have some good music on and perhaps everyone can bring something to eat (or drink). This way, you save the money for the expensive club.

Snacks between meals

The daily temptations of snacks are huge. A chocolate bar that goes with your bread bun (although the bun or croissant is probably too expensive if you buy one every day, so, perhaps bake it yourself or limit it to once a week) a doughnut with your coffee, a bag of chips in the evening, etc. If you are tempted to snack, you need a big dose of self-discipline from now on. Don't buy anything at a kiosk or in restaurants! It is best to avoid snacks and only eat at the main meals. According to interval fasting, you would also do something for your health. However, if that sounds too hard, at least buy your snacks at discount stores, and then take them with you. No spontaneous purchases on the go! For example, if you always eat the same chocolate bars, buy them in a large pack, as they are usually cheaper and take the amount you need with you every day.

Coffee

If you're a coffee lover who drinks five cups or more a day, or you need your Starbucks cappuccino every morning, a decent amount can add up throughout the year. Calculate this amount. If you're a Starbucks follower, as hard as it sounds, you should scale back your consumption and reward yourself with a

Starbucks coffee at most once a month. In the office, you may be lucky, and the coffee is free or only costs little.

However, if you buy the coffee on the go, you should consider buying a cheap machine for at home. For Starbucks coffees, you need a milk frother and possibly a caramel syrup. So, you can prepare your coffee at home. You could also bring the coffee for the day in a thermos.

Even coffee dates with friends can be moved home if you have a good machine.

Smoking

I very much hope that you can just skip this paragraph as you are already a non-smoker. We all know that smoking is simply too expensive and that nothing positive contributes to your health. So, it's best to finally stop smoking and spend half of the money saved on something else you enjoy or on something you've wanted to do for a long time. This way, you have an incentive for actually giving it up. There are countless ways to make it easier to become a non-smoker (patches, chewing gum, e-cigarettes), but the most important thing is your attitude. That you don't want to smoke anymore. If that's not possible, at least look for cheap tobacco to roll the cigarettes yourself or ask friends to bring cheap cigarettes from their holidays (for example Asia, where smoking is still possible for a few cents).

Dining out

To save money in this category, there is only one option: shop cheaply and cook yourself.
If you don't have time during the week, you should make time to pre-cook for the week on weekends. You could also arrange with your work colleagues that everyone cooks one day of the week. That way, you don't have to cook every day and your work becomes a more social place as well.

Rent

The rent is probably the biggest fixed cost point of the month. Of course, we all need a roof over our heads, but it would make a huge difference here if you suddenly paid several hundred less a month. You can consider whether you want to turn your apartment into a shared apartment so that you can split the rent and fixed costs (also internet) with roommates. If you don't have your own apartment yet, it's best to move into an existing shared apartment, as you only have to buy the furniture for your room. Maybe the room is even already furnished and otherwise, there are countless Facebook groups in which furniture is offered at very low prices or for free. Then you should also look at the location of your apartment and reconsider how many rooms you really need. Perhaps moving to a smaller apartment/a cheaper suburb would be worthwhile.

Car

Cars are a status symbol and depending on where you live, you need an Audi or BMW in order to keep up. However, driving is unfortunately a losing business. The more expensive your car is, the more you write off and the more insurance you pay. With today's possibilities, however, you no longer have to own your own car without having to give up all the comfort. Can you use carsharing in your area? Or ride by public transport or bicycle? You may also be able to share the car with neighbors, colleagues, or family. If driving is your big hobby, that's fine. Hobbies are discussed in more detail in the last sub-chapter of this chapter. You will learn how to practice your hobby without going over your budget.

Dresses, Accessories

If you're a shopping queen, you'll probably need to change your mindset a little bit. You don't need new outfits all the time and there are no-name dresses at a special offer all the time with which you can look good. Don't go shopping out of boredom or because you're feeling a little down. Give yourself a monthly budget that you can spend on clothes and accessories to keep your savings rate at 20-50%. Once you've used up this budget, you should make a big detour around department stores and online ads, so you don't get tempted to shop anymore. It would be even better not to buy monthly, but to wait for the seasonal sales and, for example, to always buy the winter fashion at the end of winter for the next year.

Dating

Especially as a man this category is tricky as it is often expected from the women to be invited by the guy for a drink or meal. Above all, at the beginning of a relationship, you probably have to spend money on dates. This is not entirely true though. Relationship researchers have found that successful relationships usually consist of partners who have met through mutual friends. This means that you don't have to go out to bars and clubs in order to meet someone. When it then comes down to going out with someone, see that you can cook at home or do something that doesn't cost much. You could go cycling, inline skating, picnicking, hiking. The only limit is your imagination. The same applies to online dating. Why do the first meetings have to be in an expensive restaurant, café, or bar? You'll probably find a better connection to each other if you're doing something active. Perhaps, for safety, the first meeting shouldn't be at someone's home, but you could surely go for a walk or a picnic in a park?

Hobbies

Hobbies are often expensive. Either you need the right equipment, the lessons are expensive, or it involves a social aspect that needs to be fulfilled. For example, you have to travel regularly to competitions with the sports club and spend the money on transport, accommodation, and food (careful with the expensive alcohol at the social events).

The good news is that it's perfectly fine to have a hobby. After all, you want to enjoy your life and use the hard-earned money for something that is fun. As a frugalist (Def.: Frugalists have the goal of being financially independent and/or retire as early as possible in life) you should limit yourself to one hobby. What is most important to you? Is it the football club, photography, the car, the instrument, ...? For this, you give yourself a monthly amount in your budget planning. This amount can also be a little higher, but then you probably have to save the money somewhere else (e.g. shopping for even cheaper groceries). What's not possible is that you have five different expensive hobbies. Living in grand style in all aspects does not fit into the attitude of a bargain hunter. Find cheap leisure activities so that you don't get bored, because if we are bored, we often tend to spend money on unnecessary things. Cheap leisure activities include walking, cycling, swimming, selling things at flea markets, watching tv, reading books (library), etc.

Savings Checklist

Category	current monthly costs	desired monthly costs	Goal achieved
Alcohol and celebrate			☐
Snacks			☐
Coffee			☐
Smoking			☐
Dining out			☐
Rent			☐
Car			☐
Dresses, Accessories			☐
Dating			☐
Hobbies			☐

Saving in every life situation

Do you think that as a poor student, a parent with young children, or a retiree, there is no way of being able to save money? Or do you think you'll never be able to save a decent amount of money anyway? These are all lazy excuses and bad dogmas.

Buying this book was your first good decision to get to a higher account balance, as you somehow believe in the possibility of saving more money. Now it's time to take the second step and really commit to a more economical lifestyle. Get an overview of your spending (with a budget app) and stop spending blindly. From now on, you should know from every penny that you earn, what you are spending it on. Then you will suddenly notice where you can easily cut back.

Above, you've learned the categories you need to look at from now on. Here are seven more tips to help you save.

1. Cheap shopping

Of course, it already helps your budget if you only shop in the cheapest stores (Lidl, Aldi, certain private vegetable shops). However, it is normal that we have our favorite products in various stores and the good news is that you don't have to completely renounce these shopping opportunities. However, you should get used to only buying discounted products. Your shopping basket should be 80% filled with special offers. 5-10% can be products you want to enjoy even though they are not discounted (just make sure that you don't overspend your shopping budget). The remaining 10% are products that you need weekly but are almost never on sale. With these products, you have to start comparing the prices in the different stores and then only buy them where they are cheapest.

The second trick to save money when shopping is to go with a shopping list and only shop with a full stomach. Then you will be less tempted to make spontaneous purchases. Plan your approximate menu at home and write down the ingredients. As I said, you can also leave room for the special offers.
Third, you should start collecting discount tokens and membership cards. As a customer, you can really benefit from these promotions.

2. Inform your social network

If you want to take saving seriously from now on, it may bring some drastic changes to your lifestyle. It is therefore important that you inform your friends and family about your savings goal.

They will certainly be happy to support you when they understand why you want to move to a different apartment or why you suddenly don't go out as often.

The five people you spend the most time with also affect you the most.
If they don't understand why you're changing your lifestyle, you might want to spend more time with people who already have the mindset of saving or are good at budgeting or investing. I, for myself, like to talk to people who have a big knowledge about the real estate market or the stock exchange. You can always learn something new or you could hear about a good deal.

3. Sharing is caring

With all the opportunities we have today to connect, it is surprising that we still live so segregated from each other and everyone needs their own kitchen utensils, garden utensils, etc.

Get a list of things you only need a few times a year and then expand the list with things you need a few times a month. These are all items you could easily share with other people. Either you buy the item together and everyone pays a part, or you can use your neighbor's lawnmower while he uses your hammock. For cars, bicycles, and scooters there are many options, especially in the cities. You no longer need your own vehicle and there is always one available near the apartment.

Some subscriptions are designed to be shared with friends (e.g. Audible or Netflix). Even if you think that it is only a few bucks per month, a large amount adds up if you remain an active customer for several years. If you don't know anyone who wants to share these services with you, you can search for people on Facebook or in internet forums. Speaking of the Internet, if you have a good relationship with your neighbors, shouldn't it be possible for you to share the Wi-Fi? After all, single-family houses don't have a separate Wi-Fi on every floor, and if you live in an apartment building and you're not a computer scientist, the speed should be enough when four or five people are on the Internet at the same time.

4. Pay immediately

You have to get used to just buying things that you can afford to pay in full. For example, it is often cheaper if you pay the health insurance amount annually and not monthly. The same applies to the purchase of a car or TV. It's just not worth leasing something, as you end up paying several hundred bucks more.
Saving money sometimes also means foregoing something or waiting until you can afford it. The

satisfaction of buying something when you know you can really afford it is much bigger anyway.
Get an overview of the big spending points that you have to pay annually (insurances, taxes, public transport card) and see that you have those sums ready until then.

5. Pay in cash

The technology works against this advice, but as long as it is still possible, get used to paying everything in cash. We spend money a lot more consciously when we physically pick up bills or coins instead of just handing out a credit or debit card. That's why you shouldn't shop on the Internet. If you want to buy something on the internet nevertheless, wait 24 hours before you buy it, and if you still need it or want to buy it, you can buy it if it fits into your budget.

6. Collect coins

Do you remember childhood days when you put your pocket money or cash gifts into your piggy bank? You'll start this again :) Use a piggy bank or any small container and get used to putting all the coins from your wallet in there every night. You probably won't notice that you don't have this money in your wallet anymore. You can also tell your friends that they can leave their excess coins in your savings box. A lot of people don't like carrying coins around with them and may be happy if they can do you a favor.

Every two to three months you bring these coins to the bank. Yes, you deposit the money into your savings account. It's not meant to be spent yet.

7. Do It Yourself

In Germany, Austria, or Switzerland, it is often cheaper to produce certain things yourself than to buy them in a shop. This can even become a fun hobby.

What you can produce yourself very well are consumer foods such as spices or oils with flavors (e.g. chili or garlic), beauty products, decorative items, and gifts. With gifts, it is all the more worthwhile to think about what personal touch would bring pleasure to the recipient. Most people can afford everything they want anyway, and a homemade but deeply thought-out gift idea means a lot.

Seductions that make saving more difficult

Although you have now set your mind firmly to achieve your savings goals, you may be falling into old patterns from time to time. Be vigilant about the following situations and then try not to make the purchase or choose a cheaper alternative. Even if it's difficult at first, you'll feel good afterward that you could resist the temptation.

Thoughts in those tempting situations could be:

- It's only a small amount

You spontaneously see something that appeals to you and since it doesn't cost much, you think it won't hurt if you buy it. Wrong, because if you have such thoughts every day, even these small amounts will add up to large sums. The fact is that you didn't actually need this item and only a momentary impulse triggered the desire for it (e.g. advertising or a delicious smell).

- I don't want to look like a penny pincher to my friends

It's not always easy to spend little money in a group if the others do not have the same attitude. However, you are not a scrooge, but you are currently taking care of your finances. If you're sick, you also have to give up sports or exercising for a while until your body is fit again.

Now your goal is to improve your account balance and even if your friends see it differently, you should stick to your goal. It is possible that you can save yourself toward financial freedom and no longer have to work as an employee in 10–15 years. You won't have to worry about how much pension your country will pay you once you are retired, as you have sufficient financial resources yourself.
Your friends, on the other hand, will still be in the same vicious circle and be at zero by mid-month, while you can still go for a beer.

- If I don't have that, I'm not trendy

If you want to save in order to become a millionaire, you should also start behaving like a typical millionaire (book: "The Millionaire Next Door" by Dr. Thomas J. Stanley and Dr. William Danko). You don't always need the latest gadgets or branded items. It is the pressure of advertising and the attitude of our consumer society that arouse the desire for an object within us. Try to ignore ads by not watching ads on the TV and not being distracted by advertisements on your PC. Maybe it would also help to read a book about minimalism so that you can understand how you can be happy without constantly possessing the latest trend.

What you should do with the saved money

"Frugality is the daughter of common sense, the sister of moderation and the mother of freedom"
- Samuel Smiles

First, you need to save up your **financial security.** You cannot be one of those people who have less than 1000 euros or dollars in their account. Your financial security is the money you need in three months. So, your monthly expenses times three. If you live cheaply in Switzerland, you can live well as a single person or couple with 2500 Fr. per person per month. Your financial security would therefore be 7500 Fr.

Now calculate this sum for your personal situation. Your first goal is to save up this amount on your savings account. You get more interest on the money in the savings account than in the account you use for your salary and expenses, even if the interest unfortunately is practically nothing in today's world. Now, if you lose your job or something unexpected happens, you know you have a three-month money cushion. That calms the nerves. You don't touch this cushion, even if you suddenly have the opportunity to buy your dream car or dream home. Otherwise, you will quickly fall into the debt trap.

Everything you save after that, you can put into different, safe investments. Hence, you divide the 20 - 50% of your saved salary into parts, which you then invest monthly or every few months. We invest in different things so that at least part of it is safe if there are problems with the financial system or the housing market. In addition, 90 % of your investments should be considered a "safe investment". You could spend 10 % of your monthly savings rate on speculative investments if you like to play with the risk. However, I am keeping away from this, as I have mostly lost money on risky investments so far.

You also have to think long-term about investing. Over the years, the money will grow and from the profits, you could then make new investments.

However, you have to bury the idea of fast money. Too often, I have seen people in our financial club jumping on a hype and then maybe quickly winning 20'000 or even 50'000 Fr. and six months or a year later they were suddenly sitting in debt. This means that even if you suddenly get a decent sum of money with your 10 % risk investments, you shouldn't let greed take hold of you and invest even more or suddenly scale your lifestyle back up to a luxury jetsetter. He who laughs last laughs best and this also applies to the slow but continuous savers.

Savings account

You should leave part of your saved money in a savings account. As has already been mentioned, there is not much interest, but it is always good to be financially liquid if an emergency emerges. However, it is advisable to store the money in different banks in case one goes bankrupt. Try to only have up to 100'000 with each bank.
Another advantage, if you have multiple accounts, is that you can benefit from the various bonus programs of the banks. Some may have a free museum pass or discounted concert tickets, etc.

Pros and cons of saving on the savings account:

+ better interest rate, you are financially fluid, and it is motivating to see how the balance increases monthly

- the money loses value due to constant inflation and is completely exposed to financial crises. Plus, from the savings account you can usually only withdraw a certain amount per quarter year (around 20'000) otherwise you have to pay extra fees.

Gold and Silver

With gold and silver, you have a fixed value that can rise sharply if there is inflation or deflation. Even if money loses its value, you will be able to trade in gold and silver as their value is more stable. That's why you should invest a small percentage of your savings rate in solid gold or silver. By solid, I mean that you pick up the metal from a gold dealer and store it at your home or in a safe at a bank. There is also the possibility to buy virtual gold, which they say they are storing somewhere for you. However, they actually sell more gold than there physically is, and if you actually want to receive the metal, you may not get it, or it will take forever until you have it. Therefore, buy precious metals physically either monthly, quarterly, or annually. As with stocks, you're more likely to compensate price fluctuations if you buy at regular intervals. Or you can compare the price and buy at a time when you think gold or silver is cheap.

The negative thing about gold or silver is that you can't generate recurring income from it. We hope that we will be able to sell it at a big profit or that it will be less exposed to inflation for the time being, but, unfortunately, in the meantime, the money is tied to the metal.

Real estate

If you had bought a property in Europe in the last 20 years, you couldn't have gone wrong. Mortgage rates in Switzerland are at 1% and the value of the property increases year after year. That is why the prices for real estate are very high at the moment. Actually, too high. However, this was probably already thought to be the case 10 years ago and yet everything still became more expensive. Here is the question of whether there will actually be a crash soon and that property prices (and also the value of houses) will fall, or whether it will continue for another 10 years. This is difficult to assess. Yet, overall, a property would be a good investment, as you can stay in it "for free" even during a financial crisis, as long as you can pay the mortgage. Calculate how much rent you pay per year for your rented apartment... It's usually worth having your own apartment or a house. Even if you do not live in it yourself, rental income is a good source of additional income, which is relatively safe and should give you an income of about 5% per year for the invested money.

On the downside, you usually need quite a lot of equity for a property and if you are just starting to save, the purchase of a property will only work if you put money on the side for it on a monthly basis. It would be quicker if you can join together with trusted people (e.g. family members) and you buy a property together. Either share the rental income fairly or you pay them a small rent.
For the time being, I would stay away from buying a property without equity, as this usually entails

much higher mortgage rates, which would then push up your monthly fixed costs again (which we want to avoid.)

ETFs

Also, at the stock market, one could only win over the last 80 years. There is always one or the other financial crisis, but in the long run, stocks have gone up. Now we are in the longest interval without a major financial crisis, leading many to believe that there will soon be an epic crash. You will find good thoughts about this in Dirk Müller's book "Powerquake: The world on the verge of the greatest economic crisis of all times – circumstances, risks, opportunities".

So, the problem would be if you buy shares now and in a few months the violent crash happens. Because then, at first, you will have lost money. However, this loss will recover at some point.
So, see stocks as a long-term investment, especially if you haven't dealt with stocks yet. In case the crash is coming soon, you should put part of your savings rate on the side so that you can invest big when all the stocks crashed. It is precisely in this case that we need liquidity.

But what are ETFs? **E**xchange-**T**raded **F**unds are investment funds, i.e. pots with different stocks that want to replicate and beat a stock index. Well-known stock indexes are the SMI (Swiss Market Index, with the largest stock companies in Switzerland) or the DAX (German Equities Index, with the 30 largest German stock companies).

You then select an ETF and buy shares in your portfolio. The ETF uses one of three methods to replicate this index. For example, the sampling method, in which he buys shares from the biggest companies.

This all runs passively once you have decided on an ETF. You don't have to study the stock market every day, but leave the money invested to grow. Another advantage of ETFs is that you don't have to pay fees for every purchase or sale of shares, which is the case with individual active trading. You pay a small, annual, or quarterly fee.

A negative point could be that you are not directly entitled to your dividends if dividends are distributed. The dividends usually buy even more shares. However, your portfolio will grow, and you will eventually make a profit.

On justetf.com (https://www.justetf.com/de/how-to/invest-in-switzerland.html) you will find ETFs in which you could invest. It even shows what your winnings might look like.

To buy ETFs, you need a stock portfolio. I would recommend that you don't do this at your regular bank, as online portfolios often have better terms.

Swissquote or **Comdirect** would be such operators.

Shares of more well-known companies

If you're interested in stocks and you're going to track prices, you're probably also interested in trading stocks yourself and not just relying on funds.

However, if you trade yourself, you should not speculate riskily. It's best to focus only on stocks from large or well-known companies (e.g. Apple, Google, Nestlé).

The second strategy would be to buy shares from companies that you (and many others you know) like. For example, if chain smokers had invested only part of their money for cigarettes in Philip Morris shares 20 years ago, they would be millionaires today. Even with Starbucks, I would have made a lot of profit if I had followed this strategy. At the moment, Amazon, Netflix, and booking.com are interesting. Which other companies can you think of?

The negative thing is that you might be buying at the wrong moment and every purchase or sale will cost you something.
The positive thing is that you can buy and sell at short notice and thus make profits over a few

days if you invest at the right moment. In addition, you will receive the dividends from the shares you keep if they pay dividends and you are allowed to go to the general assemblies that take place once a year. At the annual general meetings, you will receive interesting information and figures about the company, have a say, and usually, they serve a decent meal.

Lending loans

This proved to be the most profitable form of investment in my circle of acquaintances. It means you give a loan to trusted people and they pay you a monthly interest. Of course, they could also request a loan from the bank, but these are not easy to obtain depending on the situation they are in and secondly, these loans come with tough conditions and a lot of paperwork.

Also, with your debtor, you should set up a written contract. You can find a template for this on Financescout24.de. This contract must be respected by the debtor with regard to the amount and interest payments. Otherwise you could contact the debt enforcement office, which is not a great feeling. Therefore, weigh up well whether your borrower is creditworthy. Which means: do you think the person is able to pay you the interest regularly and will have the money back together at the end, or does the person always have problems with money anyway? Does the person have something else valuable (like a property) which you might be entitled to in an emergency?

To make it worthwhile for you, you should come up with an annual interest rate of 4% or more.

What the debtor needs the money for may not matter to you, provided you are sure that you will get your money and interest back (borrower needs a fixed income). Opportunities for credit support would be if someone wants to do expensive additional training, have to pre-finance their holiday, or make an investment.

There are also online platforms that make it easier for you to hand out loans. However, I already see this type of online investment as risky, as the platforms could close overnight. However, if you still have money left in your investment part of the budget, you could join Mintos (http://www.mintos.com/de/l/ref/CCXDPN) or Bondora (https://bondora.com/ref/BO94673K7). Start with $500. Over the last two years, I've had a 10% gain on both platforms. As I said, however, this is a less secure investment than other opportunities mentioned in this book.

Final thoughts on investment

You see, the money you save is not meant to be spent on your hobbies or dreams. Because these investments will ultimately help you grow your money much faster. You can reinvest some of your profits (e.g. dividends or rental income) or actually use it for your dreams. However, it would be a bad way of saving if you said, okay, I'll save 20'000 now and then go traveling a year and spend it all. Then, after your year of traveling, you are back at the same point as before. These dreams (e.g. travel) you have to include in your monthly budget in addition to the savings rate. I travel all the time.

Before COVID-19 I just spent 7 months in South America. But since I had budgeted my travels into every salary, I didn't come back with less money than I had before. In the past, this was only possible with shorter journeys, as I needed a regular source of income. In the meantime, however, I can live off my investments and my books, which is of course also a dream. So, it is actually cheaper for me to travel abroad and see the world than to lead a daily life in expensive Switzerland :)

If you would like to know how to make money from writing books, you can use this website: www.schreibeinbuch.wordpress.com

Sign up for a free e-mail course. At the moment the course is still in its infancy, but it should be expanded soon. So, you can be there right from the start and get fresh knowledge.

How to get more revenue in addition to investments

In order to improve your account balance even faster, instead of just relying on a life as a bargain hunter, you can of course also generate additional income through a side job.

Side job as an employee

If your main job leaves you with some free time, you can easily take on a second part-time job. This could be a kind of student job. For example, work in a bar, club, or restaurant, work in the cinema, theater, or football stadium at the box office or as an usher, bicycle courier, or product promoter. There are countless opportunities for side jobs. This was just a small selection. The great thing about side jobs is that you could combine them with a hobby. For example, I worked in the cinema for a while and, in addition to the salary, I was able to watch all the films for free. In addition, I like to go to trade fairs and have often worked at such events. This way I got to know the other people who worked there and in my free time I could stroll through the fair for free.

Secondary job as a self-employed person

Here, too, the possibilities are limitless. Most of the time, however, it's very time-consuming until you really make money as a self-employed person. That's why you should become self-employed in a field in which you are already very good or what interests you very much. For example, you could do a massage course and offer massages in a studio (or yoga, reiki, etc.), go cleaning, walk dogs or watch pets for others, bake decorative cakes for special occasions, sell items on Amazon or create a one-page shop for a popular product.

If you see potential in your main job, you could also offer additional services to other customers in your spare time. For example, as a computer scientist, or a specialist in any niche, and as a teacher, it is easy to create an opportunity.

Create a budget

Now we have reached the point where you have hopefully read this book thoroughly and given some thoughts about your finances and your savings potential. You should be able to create a realistic monthly budget with the template on the next page. Annual expenses you simply divide by 12.

Monthly budget

Month:		
Budget point	**Expected amount**	**Actual amount**
Income		
Salary from main occupation		
Salary from part-time work		
Investment income		
Total:		
Expenses		
Rent		
House/apartment additional costs (heating, water, etc.)		
Taxes		
Internet		
Phone		
Other subscriptions:		
Health insurance		
Doctor/Dentist		
Transport costs (public transport, gasoline, car insurance, etc.)		
Dining out		
Food		

Alcohol		
Snacks and coffee		
Activities (excursions, cinema, escape room, swimming pool, etc.)		
Clothes, Shoes, Accessories		
Holiday		
Other fees:		
Other acquisitions:		
Savings rate of ______ % (income minus expenses)		

How do you find this book?

If this book was helpful to you, it would mean a lot to us if you left a short, positive review on Amazon. Thank you very much! ☺

Books by partner authors that you might be interested in:

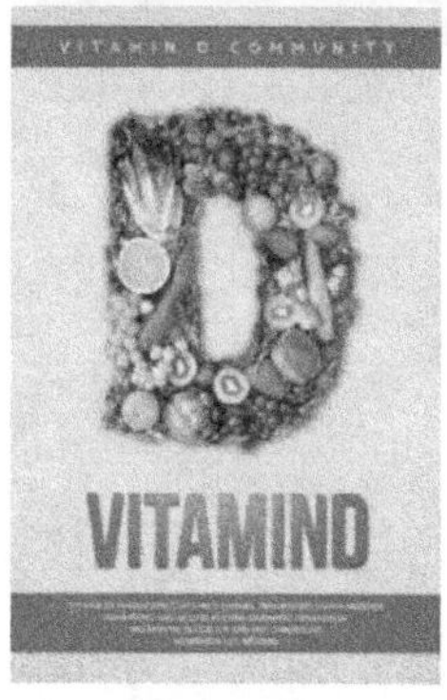

www.ingramcontent.com/pod-product-compliance
Lightning Source LLC
Chambersburg PA
CBHW060944130726
48001CB00003B/1053